CASPER'S SCARE SCHOOL

The Howling Hole

Based on the original Casper animations
Adapted by Maureen Haselhurst

Lyndhurst Primary School
Denmark House, Grove Lane,
Camberwell, SE5 8SN

Casper's Scare School

Casper
The Friendly Ghost

Mantha
The Zombie
with Style

Ra
The Funky
Mummy

Micky and Monaco
Super Stylish

Thatch
Super Mean

Hot Rod Ramses
Scary-cool Screamboarder

Ra was watching the screamboarding on TV. Hot Rod Ramses was the greatest screamboard superhero.

"Hot Rod Ramses is brilliant!" cheered Ra. "I'm going to be brave and scary-cool just like him."

"But you can't ride a screamboard," said Casper.

"Not yet," said Ra. "But I can learn!"

So Ra got a screamboard. He tried and tried and tried ...

until …

"Wow!" gasped Casper.
"You've done it!"
"And you're good!"
said Mantha.

"Ra looks just like Hot Rod Ramses in that helmet," giggled Micky.

"Hot Rod Ramses is really cool," agreed Monaco.

"You must be joking!" said Thatch. "Ra can do a few cool moves, but he's still a dummy-mummy."

"No way! I'm brave and I'm scary-cool," boasted Ra. "And to prove it, I'll … I'll screamboard across the Howling Hole!"

"Hold it, Ra! You're still learning. It's too dangerous!" Casper warned him.

Ra shrugged. "If Hot Rod Ramses can do it, then so can I."

Ra stood on the edge of the Howling Hole.

"You don't have to do this," said Casper. "Yes I do," whispered Ra. "I've got to prove that I'm not a dummy-mummy."

Ra looked into the Howling Hole. It was deep and dreadful.

"I'm scared," he said, "but *here I go*!"

Ra took a deep breath and off he went into thin air. He nearly made it across, and then he vanished ...

... Ra had fallen into the Howling Hole!

"That was silly," puffed Mantha as she and Casper pulled Ra out.

"Maybe, but it made me feel brave, like Hot Rod Ramses," said Ra.

"Hey, dummy-mummy! This is how to do it!" shouted Thatch as he swooped across the Howling Hole.

"Someone should teach Thatch a lesson," Mantha grunted.

"A lesson!" said Casper. "What a great idea!"

Dear Hot Rod Ramses,

My friend Ra wants to be a scary-cool screamboarder like you, but he's finding it a bit hard. Please can you help?

*Casper
(The Friendly Ghost)*

Soon, Scare School had a surprise visitor. It was Hot Rod Ramses!

"Looking for me?" shouted Thatch.

"No. I'm looking for a kid called Ra!" said the superhero.

"That's me!" gasped Ra.

"Fancy a screamboard lesson?" asked Hot Rod Ramses.

"Yes, please!" said Ra.

So Ra learned how to swoop and dive and twist and turn.

"Now watch," said Hot Rod Ramses and he screamboarded across the Howling Hole. "You'll do that one day," he said.

So Ra became a scary-cool screamboarder, just like Hot Rod Ramses. Maybe one day he would become a superhero too.